Benchmarking

The NETWORK, Inc., was founded in 1969 to link innovative schools in Massachusetts with one another and has developed into a highly regarded research and development organization that conducts a wide array of services designed to enhance learning. An operating principle of the organization is to create networks linking those who have knowledge with those who can use it. These paths may go from academia or the statehouse to the schoolhouse and back, from school to school, from classroom to classroom, and into the community. The work of the organization is conducted throughout the U.S. and internationally as well.

Benchmarking

A Guide for Educators

Sue Tucker
The NETWORK Inc.

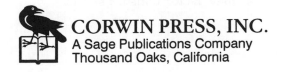

CORWIN PRESS, INC.
A Sage Publications Company
Thousand Oaks, California

For information address:

Corwin Press, Inc.
A Sage Publications Company
2455 Teller Road
Thousand Oaks, California 91320
E-mail: order@corwin.sagepub.com

SAGE Publications Ltd.
6 Bonhill Street
London EC2A 4PU
United Kingdom

SAGE Publications India Pvt. Ltd.
M-32 Market
Greater Kailash I
New Delhi 110 048 India

Printed in the United States of America

Library of Congress Cataloging-in-Publication Data

Tucker, Sue.
    Benchmarking : A guide for educators / Sue Tucker.
      p. cm.
    Includes bibliographical references.
    ISBN 0-8039-6366-1 (alk. paper). — ISBN 0-8039-6367-X (pbk. :
alk. paper)
      1. School management and organization—United States.
    2. Benchmarking—United States. I. Title.
    LB2805.T83 1995
    371.2′00973—dc20   95-24744

This book is printed on acid-free paper.

96 97 98 99 10 9 8 7 6 5 4 3 2 1

Corwin Press Project Editor: Christina M. Hill

Contents

Preface

*If there is one obvious opportunity to use bench-
marking to provide some substantial value to our
society, it is in the area of public education.*
                              —Robert Boxwell, Jr.
                                (Boxwell, 1994, p. 164)

SUCCESSFUL organizations are continually searching for
new ideas, methods, and processes to catapult them to
world-class performance. These organizations actively examine themselves as well as other organizations to learn from and
implement successful practices. *Benchmarking* is the process that
many of them use to achieve superior performance—a team research and data-driven process by which learning and innovation trigger fundamental breakthroughs in thinking and practice.
Industry has used benchmarking over the past decade to achieve
competitive advantage. As educational organizations seek to
achieve world-class standards, this process can lead the way.

This book is most timely as educators grapple with fundamental reform and restructuring. As I developed the ideas in this book, I was inspired by our conversations with many educators. The resounding message from many of them was that what's missing from school reform efforts is a careful analysis of what is and isn't working in the current system and an infusion of ideas and documented practices that work in similar settings. Furthermore, they said that all stakeholders need to be involved in this process. Too often, decisions are made and innovations selected without active involvement of those who will implement the changes. The choices are often made without data to support their being worth the investment the innovation will take. Benchmarking directly addresses these needs.

Benchmarking enables professionals to study and know their systems and continually improve their practices. As schools increasingly involve all of their stakeholders—teachers, students, parents, and community members—in the educational enterprise, they need to develop a common language to communicate what they are doing and why. The benchmarking process can be used by educators to help develop a systems view of their practices and overall organization and to set and communicate targets based on world-class operations.

This book provides step-by-step actions that improvement teams can take to (a) know their own organizations, (b) clarify which of their underlying practices and processes are most in need of attention, and (c) learn from others how to improve outcomes. It will guide its users to build a "reflection-action-reflection-action" cycle into their everyday operation. It is an important contribution to the innovative resources reformers can call on to learn about and implement world-class practices.

Acknowledgments

T HIS book is the result of the interest and efforts of many
people. I would particularly like to acknowledge Susan
Mundry, of The NETWORK, Inc.* for her enthusiasm,
support, wisdom, and knowledge of education and educators that
helped me take an idea and shape it into this book and for pa-
tiently keeping the writing moving forward.

Special thanks go to Assistant Superintendent Eleanor Ross
of Clark County, Virginia, Public Schools for sharing her school
system's experience with benchmarking.

The many reviewers and focus group participants are greatly
appreciated: Peggy Siegel, National Alliance of Business, Wash-

*The NETWORK, Inc. is a nonprofit organization founded in 1969 to link innova-
tive schools in Massachusetts with one another. It has developed into a highly
regarded research and development organization that conducts a wide array of
services designed to enhance learning. One of their operating principles is to create
networks linking those who have knowledge with those who can use it. These paths
may go from academia or the statehouse to the schoolhouse and back, from school
to school, from classroom to classroom, and into the community. Their work is
conducted throughout the United States and internationally as well.

ington, D.C.; Thomas Trant, Minnesota Academic Excellence Foundation; Arlyene Alexander, Total Quality Education Institute of the Connecticut Business and Industry Association, Hartford; Superintendent Ronald Fitzgerald and Assistant Superintendent Beverly Lydiard, Minuteman Science Technology High School, Lexington, Massachusetts; Total Quality Consultant Carol Bershad, Natick, Massachusetts; Craig Stanley, Greater Lawrence Education Collaborative, Lawrence, Massachusetts; Superintendent George Blaisdell, North Andover Schools, North Andover, Massachusetts; and Joseph Giordano, Whittier Vocational Technical School, Lawrence, Massachusetts.

Thanks go to Denise Blumenthal, David Crandall, Nancy Love, and Sue Martin, staff members from The NETWORK, Inc. in Andover, Massachusetts, who reviewed many drafts of the book and contributed their knowledge and expertise as it was developed.

Special appreciation is due Doris Sipowicz, Jennifer Bertrand, and Lynne Murray at The NETWORK, Inc. for their assistance in preparing the final manuscript.

And last, I wish to express my appreciation to Bob Boxwell, author of *Benchmarking for Competitive Advantage,* for his encouragement of educators and this project to transfer benchmarking to education.

Sue Tucker
September 1995

From the Author

WHEN was the last time you read, saw, or heard about an intriguing curriculum, management system, or instructional method reaping superior results in another school (system)?

How many times did you think to yourself, "That's exactly what we need in our school (system) to really get serious about implementing those improvement goals we set last year"?

And how often did you rapidly dismiss the thought because "that great idea could never work in our school"?

Benchmarking is about changing this last line from "it could never work in our school" to "we know how to examine that other school's best practice, measure the results, and adapt it to our school."

Because I have one foot in education, another foot in business, and a hand in politics, the principles of benchmarking are especially compelling to me. The foundation of benchmarking is education—transferring learning from one group to another group. The process, methods, and language of benchmarking have roots in business and in quality management. International competition forced U.S. industry to develop a method of quickly finding and implementing world-class practices that achieved world-class results. The alternative to this was, quite simply, to perish. Politically, I know that U.S. schools are facing similar pressures for higher levels of achievement and accountability from all levels of government as well as from taxpayers, employers, and parents.

If you are reading this guide, you are probably a risk taker who is willing to look everywhere—even to other disciplines and sectors—for ideas to improve education. You already understand the need for educators to get "outside the box" and challenge business as usual on every front.

Most likely, you also understand the barriers and difficulties in adopting so-called business language and practices to education. The "not invented here" syndrome is a powerful barrier to learning. As the author, I make no apologies for using the language of quality in the guide. More and more schools are learning this terminology and achieving some degree of comfort with it. Quality is the language of America's economic survival.

At the same time, I acknowledge the difficulty and the challenge that this terminology represents to educators whose training and experience have reinforced the conclusion that schools and businesses live on different planets. Therefore, I have prepared an "at-a-glance" glossary of the basic principles of quality as they relate to education and as they appear in this guide; you'll find it following this section. Your benchmarking team may want to review and discuss the glossary to ensure a common vocabulary.

A primary motivation for writing this book is my unyielding belief that good ideas from business ought not go to waste in education and vice versa. America's future absolutely depends on educators who insist on lifelong learning and continuous improvement—for themselves and for their students. Lifelong learning dictates that we challenge the mind-set "we have always done it this way" and learn from the "best of the best" wherever it is found.

At-a-Glance
Quality Glossary

Continuous Improvement Regardless of what data tell you about how your school currently performs—whether you are very high or very low on a scale—everything in your school can get better and better. Every single process—learning, teaching, discipline, food service, assessment, professional development, and so forth—can be continuously improved by people working together using quality improvement methods.

Customers The individuals and groups that receive your work. Whether it is a parent attending a parent-teacher conference or an employer in your community who hires your graduates, someone is the recipient of your efforts, both in the short term and over time. The degree to which you meet their needs and expectations defines the quality of your work. Focusing on the customer is a basic principle of quality management.

Many educators are more comfortable with the word *stakeholder* than with the word *customer.* Although I believe that the use of the word customer forces far more clarity about who is actually receiving the output of your work, I do not believe that substituting the word stakeholder undermines the benchmarking process; use it if resistance to the word customer gets in the way of learning.

Data and Performance Measures You can and must measure how well you are meeting your customers' expectations in all aspects of your school (system). Guessing doesn't count.

Teamwork Continuous improvement depends on teamwork. Everyone has a piece of the improvement puzzle and all of these pieces are related. Teachers, guidance personnel, administrators, students, employers, parents, the school board, and support staff members are all customers and suppliers to each other at one time or another. If they work in isolation or at cross-purposes, it is impossible to improve outcomes.

Introduction

About This Guide
and Your Benchmarking Project

Benchmarking: A Guide for Educators is designed to lead a team step by step through the benchmarking process, from deciding what to benchmark to implementing the selected practice. Each of the nine chapters represents an important step in the learning process and builds on the previous sessions. Therefore, it is important to follow the guide sequentially. Each chapter contains a purpose statement, background information on the step, and exercises designed to assist the team in applying that step to its particular project. Common questions dealt with in the guide include the following:

- How long will a benchmarking project take from beginning to completion?
- How often and how long should the benchmarking team meet during the project?
- Should we use a benchmarking consultant or should we "go it alone"?

All of these questions are related, and all of the answers depend on a number of variables that are best illustrated in two scenarios.

Scenario A: A successful 3-month benchmarking project on a specific practice in which little or no outside facilitation or consulting expertise was necessary.

One of Jefferson High's strategic goals was to develop a school-based enterprise to integrate and apply business and technology curriculum and skills in a school-to-work initiative. Administrators, teachers, guidance personnel, business advisers, the school board, parents, and students worked together to establish a benchmarking team to locate, study, and adapt the characteristics of the most successful school-based enterprises in the country to their school.

The team worked well together and shared a common sense of purpose. Teamwork was encouraged, and members had experience in group dynamics and problem solving. When disagreements emerged regarding performance measures, the team was able to work through the conflict without significant delays.

Because school leaders were committed both to the school-based enterprise and to learning how to benchmark, administrators arranged a 2-day summer retreat for the team to plan its study, document current practices, and develop a research plan to locate and select a benchmarking partner. The team leader was provided some release time during the fall semester for her responsibilities in coordinating the project.

When school began in the fall, the team met for 2 hours every week to share research information and develop their site visit questionnaire. The site visit they selected was within a 4-hour drive, in a neighboring state, and arranged for mid-October. After the visit, the team again met in weekly 2-hour sessions to analyze the information collected and adopt a set of recommendations for the school. By late November, the recommendations had been widely communicated and the school was well on its way to writing an action plan for implementation in the next school year. The time span was 3.5 months from beginning to completion.

Scenario B: A less successful, 14-month benchmarking project on a very broad issue in which outside facilitation would have saved both time and money.

Central Urban School System recognized that it needed a coherent, systemwide approach to violence prevention. Safety had become the number one concern of parents and the primary reason the schools were losing students to private or parochial schools. The superintendent unilaterally selected a group of people to "go benchmark violence prevention programs." With the exception of two members, this group had never worked together before, nor had they had training in team-building skills. In fact, there was historic distrust among several members stemming from a redistricting plan 2 years prior. Some members were defensive about violence prevention in general because they felt that they were already doing everything possible to reduce violence in their schools and that benchmarking measures would be "used against them."

The team spent the first 2-hour meeting just trying to (a) figure out when and where to meet and (b) answer the question, "What are we doing here?" They concluded that one 3-hour morning meeting a month was all the time they could afford for the project.

The team's first meeting was a signal of what was to come. When they began to study and document current practices, members were unable to get beyond their individual school's discipline practices to analyze the entire system. They spent a great deal of time in side conversations assigning blame for their current problems to certain individuals and groups. They asked, "Why are we doing this? We already know the problem is the parents." Or they said, "Joe Johnson in central office is the problem. Get rid of him and we would fix the whole discipline process!" Cliques developed on the team.

Even well into the third month, the team could not begin its research on potential benchmarking partners because members could not agree on what criteria to use. Some members absolutely discounted looking at any school system that had different demographics or a larger budget, regardless of its performance measures in violence prevention.

Six months after convening, a benchmarking partner was finally selected and the questionnaire drafted. Though still polarized, a central core of members felt they were making progress. Excitement was growing because of what they were learning—entirely new approaches to violence prevention were opening up to them through their partner.

The team learned, however, that no money had been budgeted for a site visit, which required $330.00 for plane tickets. Three more months passed before the money was released. School board members were suspicious of out-of-state travel for a project they knew nothing about.

Several months after the site visit, the benchmarking team did in fact develop a compelling set of recommendations for Central Urban Schools based on the excellent outcomes of its partner's practices in violence prevention. An action plan to implement the priority recommendations was being drafted in each school in the district. The time span was 14 months from beginning to completion.

The variables in these two scenarios, which clearly affected both the length of the project and the need for outside assistance, include the following:

- The scope of the issue selected for benchmarking
- The degree of commitment to the project exhibited by the top leadership that in turn determines
- The amount of resources allocated to the project and the number of barriers that are removed for the team
- The training and experience in teamwork skills and team leadership that exist in the group
- The degree to which team members understand the project as *learning activity* instead of as *punishment activity* for poor performance
- The extent to which the benchmarking project and its expected outcomes are understood by the team and the administration
- The diversity of stakeholder groups involved in the initial planning of the project

About the Author

SUE TUCKER is a quality management consultant and trainer specializing in education, government, and nonprofit applications of quality management. She is a Regional Councilor for the Education Division of the U.S. Society of Quality Control and a member of the Massachusetts Council for Quality Education.

An Associate of GOAL/QPC—a quality management training, consulting, and publishing company—she helped design and write a comprehensive *Total Quality Management in Education Series* to assist educators in learning about and implementing quality management. She adapted the "Management and Planning Tools of Quality" for schools in *The Educator's Companion to the Memory Jogger Plus* + produced by GOAL/QPC.

For 8 years, she served in the Massachusetts legislature as a state representative and vice chair of the Education Committee, which is responsible for all state laws and funding of public education, kindergarten through university levels. She was the author of numerous bills in the areas of professional development, education partnerships, school finance, and at-risk youth.

In 1989, she was an International Fellow to the European Community, sponsored by the European Parliament in Strasbourg, France, studying how education and work-training policies contribute to the economies of European countries. She has taught Women in Politics courses at Tufts University and in the secondary schools of Lexington and Andover, Massachusetts.

1

What Is Benchmarking?

*Benchmarking is the search for best practices that lead
to superior performance.*

—Robert Camp, benchmarking
pioneer and author
(Camp, 1989, p. 12)

THE PURPOSE OF THIS CHAPTER IS
to provide an overview of the definition, purpose, benefits,
and process of benchmarking as it is practiced today in
organizations worldwide. The context of this overview is
education: how benchmarking can be adapted from industry and used for school improvement.

BECAUSE benchmarking is a team rather than an individual project, it is important for several people in each set-
ting to understand its meaning, purpose, and potential
applications in their own school or school system. The exercise at
the conclusion of the chapter is designed to facilitate group discussion on the information in this chapter.

1

Two Definitions of Benchmarking

The dictionary defines benchmarking as "A surveyor's mark . . . of a previously determined position . . . used as a reference point . . . a standard by which something can be measured or judged" (Camp, 1989, p. 12).

The *Superintendent's Quality Challenge* says,

> Benchmarking is an improvement process in which an organization compares its performance against best-in-class organizations, determines how those organizations achieved their performance levels, and uses the information to improve its own performance: the subjects that can be benchmarked include strategies, products/programs/services, operations, processes and procedures. (Pinellas County Schools, 1994, p. 29)

What Is or Is Not Benchmarking?

Benchmarking is not a general measurement of your school against another school. Instead, it is the study and transfer of specific exemplary practices, measures, and processes from another school or organization to your school.

It is not this: "Let's see how we compare to school *X*." Rather, it is this:

> Reducing violence is most important to our stakeholders and a major goal in our strategic plan. Let's find the school or organization that has had the most success in reducing violence, study and analyze how they achieved success, and adapt those practices in our school.

Or it can be this:

> Implementing quality management throughout our school system is our main strategy for decentralizing to school-

based management. We will identify the school system that has demonstrated the best measurable outcomes from quality management and study their implementation process and practices.

Benchmarking is not a suggestion system or mechanism for adopting the countless small improvement ideas that individuals learn about in journals or at conferences. These can be implemented without benchmarking. Benchmarking is linked to a school's critical improvement goals, such as violence prevention, technology-assisted instruction, school-based management, school-work curriculum integration, and so forth.

Benchmarking is not a quick review or a "look and see tour" of another school's good program. It is a study of everything that contributes to the positive outcomes in a school that has the very best outcomes in a particular education arena.

Benchmarking is not a mechanism for reducing the school budget. Instead, it is a mechanism for deploying resources in the most effective manner to achieve customer (stakeholder) satisfaction.

Benchmarking is not a cookbook program that requires only a recipe for success. Instead, it is a discovery and learning process that can be used over and over again to achieve different goals. It is a way of working and thinking in the school to achieve continuous improvement. See Table 1.1 for examples of what benchmarking is and is not.

Educators are not strangers to the concept of exemplary practices. A tremendous pool of knowledge is available regarding what works in schools. Numerous journals, organizations, and conferences are devoted to "best practices" in education and expose administrators, teachers, and board members to hundreds of examples of extraordinary school success each year.

The federal government supports national clearinghouses on topics such as science education, early childhood education, and many more. The National Diffusion Network identifies, validates, and disseminates best practices and links them with potential users. Best practices information systems are also in place at the state level.

Table 1.1 Benchmarking

Is Not	Is
A general comparison of your school to another school	The study and transfer of specific best practices
A method of making little improvements "here and there"	Linked to your school's vision and critical goals
Based on "best guesses" of what might work	Based on actual performance measures
A "look-see" review of another school's program	An in-depth analysis of processes, data, and enablers
A mechanism for cutting the budget	A mechanism for achieving stakeholder satisfaction
A cookbook program with standard success recipes	A discovery and learning process
Changing for the sake of change	Thorough preparation and articulation of the goals for change

The problem is not lack of information about exemplary practices: The problem is bringing the learning home and making it work in your school or school system. Because of competitive pressures and the mandate to "improve or perish," U.S. businesses were forced to learn quickly how to identify best practices and to implement them in their own companies. Quality management principles and tools provided the framework, the language, and the methods for transferring best practices from one organization to another. Educators can learn a great deal from industry about how this comes together through benchmarking.

The History of Benchmarking:
Where It Came From and How It Evolved

Most of us are familiar with the famous Japanese business visits to American companies in the 1960s and 1970s. Within a short time, those Japanese visitors had returned home, implemented, and improved on the processes and practices they had seen in America. How is it possible to transfer learning across organizations and across cultures so efficiently and rapidly? Basically, the Japanese used the following commonsense strategies to transfer learning, which evolved into the benchmarking process:

- They came in teams so that many eyes and minds studied the way things were accomplished.
- They knew their own practices thoroughly before visiting others. Only by understanding what, how, when, who, and why you perform your own work can you understand the performance of others.
- They understood their own measures and goals so they could ask the right questions: How many hours or days does this process take? How does the process flow between and among departments and staff? Who supplies the best equipment for doing this? How many hours of training do you provide? What is the cost?
- They involved the total organization in implementing improvements back home. The managers and the workers affected by changes were directly involved in the benchmarking study and the implementation of the learning derived from it.

Benchmarking evolved in America in the early 1980s when global competition forced American industry to find methods of rapidly improving products and services or else face extinction. Quality management was spreading rapidly, and it provided managers with new principles, tools, and methods for analyzing the way people and processes worked in their businesses.

Xerox Corporation is certainly one of the foremost benchmarking pioneers in the United States; their success story is examined in detail in many of the benchmarking books listed in the Suggested Reading section. Other companies, such as Federal Express and IBM, had such extraordinary, measurable outcomes from learning and using benchmarking that it has become a common business practice that is constantly being refined, improved, and adapted for nonmanufacturing applications as diverse as health care and hotels. Almost all of the Fortune 500 companies have done at least one benchmarking project, and many use the process on a regular basis. In 1989, the Massachusetts Institute of Technology Commission on Productivity reported that "a characteristic of all best-practice U.S. firms, large or small, is an emphasis on benchmarking: comparing the performance of their products and work processes with those of world leaders in order to achieve improvement and measure progress" (Boxwell, 1994, p. 37). Benchmarking is an important part of the Malcolm Baldrige National Quality Award (1994), and organizations competing for it are required to document their benchmarking projects in several sections of the application. Instituted by the U.S. Congress in 1987, this award recognized quality achievement and excellence. All privately or publicly held companies are eligible.

In 1995, after 2 years of research and input by educators and organizations such as the Association for Supervision and Curriculum Development and the American Association of School Administrators, information about the upcoming Baldrige Quality Award for Education was released. Many leaders expect that it will radically change the way we assess school effectiveness. Schools that are pioneers in benchmarking will be on the leading edge of the Baldrige quality assessment process.

Industry does not look only to competitors or businesses that "look like them" for best practices. As Table 1.2 illustrates, they often look outside their own sector for ideas.

Benchmarking Examples in Business and Industry: "Look Everywhere for Best Practices"

The assumption in this guide is that educators will begin benchmarking in the education sector. As skills and knowledge increase, we hope that it will become common practice for schools

Table 1.2 Benchmarking Examples in Business and Industry:
Look Everywhere for Best Practices

Benchmarked	Company	Best Practice
Xerox	American Express	Collection process
	L.L. Bean	Distribution process Order fulfillment
	Marriott	Customer survey techniques
	Miliken	Employee recognition
Motorola	Domino's Pizza	Cycle time between order and delivery
Ford	Mazda	Accounts payable

to benchmark on a broader scale and look to other sectors for world-class measures and practices. Benchmarking projects that can reach outside education and into other sectors might include the following:

- How do leading edge organizations use technology to enhance learning and communication?
- What are the success measures and processes used by industry for training and professional development?
- How do publishers reduce the cycle time from idea to product?
- How do the best community coalitions build consensus among diverse stakeholders?

How Does Benchmarking Fit Into Existing School Improvement Efforts?

The following are some examples of how schools and school systems can use benchmarking to assess their already existing efforts:

Examples

- Schools engaged in strategic planning can use bench-marking to rapidly address specific strategic goals in their plans.
- School improvement councils or teams charged with im-plementing site-based management can use benchmark-ing to prevent "wheel reinvention" and learn how other organizations have addressed the issues they are facing.
- *GOALS 2000* and higher standards of achievement and accountability required by both state and federal law mean that schools will have to use faster and more effec-tive methods of improving curricula, instruction, learn-ing outcomes, and programs.
- Federal and state mandates, such as school-to-work or alternative assessment, can be implemented more effi-ciently through a benchmarking study.
- Schools learning about quality management and process improvement can establish benchmarking teams to in-crease their understanding of quality principles and tools.
- Schools and school systems deeply engaged in quality assessment can practice one of the fundamental improve-ment strategies required in the Malcolm Baldrige Qual-ity Award criteria.

An Overview
of Benchmarking Methodology

Several benchmarking models have evolved in the past few years, all with slightly different arrangements or slants on the process. The basic components of each model are, however, uni-versal and designed to answer the questions shown in Table 1.3, resulting in self-knowledge and an understanding of why and how the "best of the best" got that way.

This book will lead you step by step through each of the com-ponents shown in Table 1.4.

Table 1.3 Benchmarking Methodology Answers These Questions

What are you doing?	What are they doing?
How are you doing it?	How are they doing it?
How well are you doing it?	How well are they doing it?
Why are we getting our results?	Why are they getting their results? (What are the conditions and enablers?)

SOURCE: Xerox Corporation. Used by permission.

Table 1.4 The Benchmarking Process Contains These Components

Plan your study: Identify what to benchmark and select your team.

Study and document your own practices, success measures, and problems.

Identify best practices and establish your benchmarking partnership.

Develop a questionnaire and a process to study and document your partner's practices.

Analyze the information: the gap between you and your partner, the enablers, and the best ideas to emerge from the study.

Develop recommendations to adapt the learning to your own school and widely communicate your findings.

Implement the recommendations and monitor progress.

Stop Here and Complete Exercise 1.1

EXERCISE 1.1

1. Assemble a small, diverse team of people, such as teachers, administrators, school board members, parents, and so forth, in your school or school system to read this chapter.
2. Discuss the following questions and record comments on a worksheet patterned after Table 1.5. Based on this overview of benchmarking, what are some of the
   - positive aspects (+),
   - questions (?) it raises, and
   - negative aspects (–) of pursuing it in our school or school system?

Table 1.5 Sample Worksheet

Based on this overview of benchmarking, what are some of the positive aspects (+), the questions (?), and the negative aspects (–) of pursuing it in our school or school system?

+	?	–

2

Should Your School Begin Benchmarking?

Prerequisites, Considerations, and Cautions

*If you always do what you always did, you will always
get what you always got.*

—Anonymous

> THE PURPOSE OF THIS CHAPTER IS
> to present a realistic picture of the resources, the skills,
> and the leadership necessary to successfully complete a
> benchmarking project.

THE first chapter explained the advantages and excellent benefits many organizations have derived from benchmarking. Table 2.1 illustrates in more detail the potential advantages of benchmarking that must be weighed against the cautions and considerations presented in this chapter.

11

Table 2.1 Advantages of Benchmarking for School Improvement

Without Benchmarking	With Benchmarking
"We have always done it this way"	Challenge to business as usual: *breakthrough thinking*
Problems in the school are intractable	Understanding, by example, that improvement is possible
Start from scratch and reinvent the wheel	Learn from others for faster, more efficient improvements
New practices dictated from above and imposed on people	Teams of people study and implement new practices based on their own learning
Lack of measures to determine the success of new practices	Establish and document goals and performance measures
Blame people for lack of successful outcomes	Focus on the enablers that lead to successful outcomes in other schools
"Stop and go" haphazard improvement efforts	Planned process for sustained attention to improvement

This chart illustrates the "good news" about benchmarking. The "bad news" is not found in the outcomes but in the difficulty of actually working through a deceptively simple process. It is hard work, and there are important prerequisites and cautions to consider before embarking on a benchmarking study. The Benchmarking Readiness Assessment, found at the conclusion of this chapter, should be used and analyzed by a cross section of people (administrators, faculty, staff) in your school before you embark on a project.

Within corporations, both individual divisions and departments and corporatewide teams use benchmarking methodology on a regular basis. Likewise in education, benchmarking projects can be school based or systemwide, depending on the process selected and the degree of autonomy granted within the system to individual schools. To illustrate and assess the prerequisites and cautions, a school-based project is referenced in this chapter; the same issues apply to systemwide projects, although some language change is necessary to reflect this application.

Learning From
Experienced Organizations

A recent survey by the American Productivity and Quality Center (1992, p. 87) asked the following question of numerous organizations with considerable benchmarking histories: "In your company's experience, when a benchmarking study and implementation are not successful, to what extent are the following factors the cause?"

The top four causes of failure stood out from the rest by a considerable margin:

Top Failure Causes

- Poor planning
- No top management support
- No process owner involvement (i.e., the people most affected by potential changes were not included in the project)
- Insufficient benchmarking skills

Few school systems—or organizations of any type—would rate themselves highly on all of these items.

Prerequisites to Benchmarking

The following six prerequisites are not intended to discourage benchmarking but rather to provide guidance on factors that are likely to affect your success with the process.

1. Top administrators and leaders in the school and school system, including the school board, have an understanding of and commitment to benchmarking and continuous improvement.

The purpose and benefits of benchmarking must be understood by administrators. As the survey indicated, top management's lack of commitment to the project is one of the leading causes of benchmarking failure. Of course, real expertise comes only through practice. To get started, it is only necessary that the basic methodology and purpose be understood and that a real commitment is made to the process.

- Only administrators can allocate the necessary resources to make the project successful.
- Only administrators can establish the school climate that gives the benchmarking team the permission and power to act on their learning.

2. The school has a clear mission and has identified specific improvement goals through strategic or long-range planning. There is shared knowledge and agreement on these goals as well as on the strengths and weaknesses of the school.

Benchmarking must be linked to specific improvement goals or it will be a waste of resources. Without widespread agreement on goals among stakeholders, the changes necessary to implement benchmarking learning won't happen.

3. The school has a culture of teamwork.

Benchmarking is a team project. Participants need a basic understanding of the behaviors and skills necessary to make a team function smoothly. Although team skills are developed and enhanced during a benchmarking project, this is not the place to begin for schools that have no history of solving problems by working together.

4. The school has some experience in problem solving and process management; instead of always blaming people, the school looks for improvement opportunities.

The benchmarking team needs to be able to identify and analyze the "who, what, when, where, why" components of a specific practice in their school and their partner's school, such as curriculum development or the use of technology. Instead of blaming people, either specific individuals or groups of individuals (e.g., teachers, administrators, parents, students) for existing problems, they will examine all of the factors that influence the practice they are studying, such as policies, procedures, training, equipment, and materials.

Essentially, benchmarking requires an *improvement mind-set*, which reaches for solutions in the process, versus a *blame mind-set*, which views problems as the hopeless failures of people in the system.

5. Training and professional development is highly valued in the school by both administrators and staff.

Benchmarking requires people to learn new skills, and the school needs a tradition of recognizing and rewarding learning at all levels.

6. School-based management and decision making has progressed to the degree necessary for school teams to implement changes.

If the school system is still operating under rigid, bureaucratic, top-down rules that protect and ensure the status quo, benchmarking will not result in improvements.

Time and Cost Considerations

Benchmarking requires substantial investment of both human and financial resources. In schools, this will most certainly require redirecting some current professional development and school improvement resources. Of course, organizations that obtain breakthrough improvements through benchmarking will argue that it is the best possible investment of resources and that quality is always less expensive than poor results and stakeholder dissatisfaction.

There are many variables in trying to assess how much time and money to set aside for a benchmarking project; these will be discussed in more detail in the next chapter. Some time and cost variables include the following:

- How much training will be needed
- How much in-house or pro bono expertise is available
- How often and how long the team will meet
- How advanced the school's understanding is of its strategic goals and existing practices
- How complicated the issue selected for benchmarking is
- How easy or difficult it is to find a partner to work with you within your time frame
- How expensive it will be to visit your benchmarking partner

Some General Resource Guidelines

School Personnel

- One team leader working at 15% of a full-time job for 6 months
- Five or six team members meeting three times a month for 6 months (consider release time—cost of substitutes, etc.)
- Clerical staff and research assistance 4 hours per week for 6 months

Training and Consulting Fees

- 2-day on-site training for your team: approximately $3,000
- Ongoing consulting support: approximately $1,500 per day (I urge you to develop and use in-house or pro bono expertise wherever possible.)

Travel Expenses

- Number of on-site visits times the number of team members traveling (varies according to destination and accommodations)
- Some benchmarking projects can be accomplished via phone and fax—clearly less expensive than site visits. This alternative is addressed in Chapter 6.

As you can see, personnel, training, and travel expenses can easily exceed $10,000 for an initial benchmarking project. The resources required illustrate again the need for top management's commitment to the project. Future benchmarking studies will be less expensive because you can rely on the in-house expertise you have developed during your initial project and you will be able to move through the process with more confidence.

Stop Here and Complete Exercises 2.1 and 2.2

EXERCISE 2.1:
Benchmarking Readiness Assessment

Be certain that the group using this instrument represents a cross section of the school community (e.g., administrators, teachers, staff, and other stakeholders likely to participate in a benchmarking study). Pattern your assessment worksheets after Table 2.2.

1. Ask each person to fill out the assessment individually, indicating their personal assessment of how the school or school system rates on each issue.
2. Have the group then discuss each item and reach consensus on a number that best represents the current rating in the school or school system.

Table 2.2 Sample Assessment Worksheet

---

1. Administrators who are potentially affected by benchmarking understand its basic methodology, purpose, and potential benefits.

   5   4   3   2   1

2. The school board has been briefed on benchmarking and has indicated support.

   5   4   3   2   1

3. Administrators have a plan for allocating resources to benchmarking.

   5   4   3   2   1

4. The school has developed clear mission and vision statements.

   5   4   3   2   1

5. Specific, measurable improvement goals for the school have been established.

   5   4   3   2   1

6. There is widespread agreement on these improvement goals within the internal and external school communities.

   5   4   3   2   1

7. Teamwork is an important part of the school culture.

   5   4   3   2   1

8. People from different departments, grade levels, or schools often work together to achieve common goals.

   5   4   3   2   1

9. Improvement suggestions are actively solicited and acted on.

   5   4   3   2   1

Table 2.2 (Continued)

10. People who take risks and try new ideas are supported and encouraged.

        5   4   3   2   1

11. Training and professional development programs are strongly emphasized at the school.

        5   4   3   2   1

12. The school has had some training in teamwork, problem solving, process management, and quality management.

        5   4   3   2   1

13. High expectations and the belief that improvement is possible are projected and reinforced in the school's day-to-day operations.

        5   4   3   2   1

14. Barriers to change are being reduced and removed in the school. We have implemented change in the past.

        5   4   3   2   1

NOTE: 5 = Excellent—applies in almost all cases; 3 = OK—tolerable but could use improvement; 1 = poor—very rarely applies.

EXERCISE 2.2:
Analyzing the Results

This assessment is designed to assist schools in making sound decisions about proceeding with a benchmarking project. There is no specific score that represents a green light or a red light. If both individual and consensus scores are low on the scale in certain areas, a warning light is clearly flashing for attention to those issues.

For example, if you scored "teamwork" low—Items 7 and 8 on the worksheet—you should consider team-building training before embarking on a benchmarking project. Likewise, if the school lacks shared improvement goals—Items 5 and 6 on the worksheet—you should consider strategic planning or schoolwide goal development so you can link your benchmarking efforts to those goals.

Ask the group to discuss the following questions in the order given:

1. Are there significant differences in perception among the various stakeholders in the group (i.e., teachers, administrators, parents)?
2. If so, how can these discrepancies be explained?
3. Are there particular areas we need to address before we begin benchmarking? If so, brainstorm a list of strategies and actions to take in the next 6 months to increase your score.

Resources related to these questions can be found in the Suggested Readings list.

3

===

Planning Your Benchmarking Project

Learning organizations . . . [are those] where people continually expand their capacity to create the results they truly desire, where new and expansive patterns of thinking are nurtured, where collective aspiration is set free, and where people are continually learning how to learn together.

—Peter Senge (quoted in Belden, Hyatt, & Ackley, 1993, p. 3)

THE PURPOSE OF THIS CHAPTER IS to assist you in organizing your project by leading you through the following steps:

- Decide what to benchmark
- Select your team
- Organize your project by writing a team charter

Remember that the survey respondents in Chapter 2 ranked poor planning as the number one cause of benchmarking failure. The tools and exercises in this chapter will not only facilitate your planning process but also build teamwork and experience with quality planning tools.

Deciding What to Benchmark

The first step is to determine what to benchmark. The benchmarking team cannot be selected prior to selecting the topic because the choice of team members is driven by knowledge of the issue. The expertise of those closest to the selected issue will be essential to the study and the implementation of the results.

One of the definitions of benchmarking cited in Chapter 1 states, "the subjects that can be benchmarked include strategies, products/programs/services, processes, and procedures." This definition is intended to encourage broad thinking about potential topics. Most issues fall into two or more categories, and it is unnecessary to define your choice as a process, a service, or a strategy. Some issues are, in fact, "all of the above" depending on the scope and dimensions of the study.

Who Decides What to Benchmark?

In organizations that use benchmarking on a regular basis, the project is often initiated at a departmental or "grassroots" level. Initial or pilot projects, however, are usually identified by a management team or quality steering council according to the guidelines given in Table 3.1.

Examples of Benchmarking Topics

Strategic Planning

- Site-based management and budgeting
- School-to-work initiatives
- Quality management implementation
- Technology use to improve learning

Table 3.1 Characteristics of a Good Benchmarking Topic

The issue is a strategic goal for school improvement.

The goals for improvement can be articulated and measured.

Internal or external customer satisfaction or dissatisfaction with the current practice is well-known and well-documented (e.g., accreditation weakness, internal or external customer complaints, etc.).

You have—or can obtain—performance measures.

Federal and state mandates suggest that change in this area is now, or soon will be, an imperative.

Families seek alternatives (e.g., private schools, other public schools, home schooling, etc.) based on perceived strengths or weaknesses in the area.

NOTE: Criteria for selecting your first project ought to include an issue that has *high success potential within a designated time frame*. Unless you clearly understand that you are doing top-level, strategic benchmarking for long-term change, an issue that is too broad or too overwhelming will result in frustration.

Operations

- Scheduling and extension of school day or year
- Transportation or food service (linked to customer satisfaction and cost)

Programs and Services

- Reading, mathematics, science, and so forth
- Curriculum and instruction
- Violence prevention programs
- Professional development linked to improvement goals
- Bilingual education

Process and Procedures

- Team teaching
- Inclusion
- Portfolio assessment
- Discipline process

Stop Here and Complete Exercise 3.1

EXERCISE 3.1:
The Decision Matrix

1. Brainstorm a list of potential benchmarking issues and list them down the left column of the blank matrix worksheet. See Table 3.2 for the suggested layout.

Table 3.2 Decision Matrix Worksheet

CRITERIA	Criterion 1	Criterion 2	Criterion 3	Criterion 4	Criterion 5	Total Score
OPTIONS						
1.						
2.						
3.						
4.						
5.						

NOTE: For total score, enter rank times weight totals across all columns.

2. Develop a list of criteria that are important to you in selecting the issue and list them across the top row. Examples of criteria to consider include the following:

   - The issue is important to internal customers (i.e., stakeholders such as students and teachers within the school).
   - The issue is important to external customers (i.e., stakeholders such as parents and employers outside the school).
   - The potential for successful change in the area is high.
   - There is commitment to allocate resources (i.e., time and money) to the issue within the school community.
   - Specific improvement goals and measures can be articulated (i.e., "We know what we want to achieve through change in this area").
   - Progress is likely within a certain time frame (6 months, 1 year, etc.).

☞ *TIP: Criteria must reflect desired outcomes and be able to give you relative ranks. For example, "cost" is not a good criterion, whereas "low cost" is, because it reflects the desired outcome and can be compared among various options. Likewise, "time" is not a good criterion but "achievable within 1 year" is, because you can rank the extent to which the options meet it.*

---

3. Ask each team member to weight each criterion, distributing the value of 1.0 among the criteria. Think of this as "spending a dollar" on them all: One criterion may be worth 25 cents, whereas another may be worth 15 cents. Enter the team's combined weighting for each criterion on the matrix.
4. As a team, rank the extent to which each option meets each criterion. The option that best meets the criterion is assigned the highest rank. For reference, look at Table 3.3, a partially completed decision matrix. In the sample, there are five options: The option that best meets the criterion is assigned a 5; the option that least meets the criterion is assigned a 1.

Table 3.3 Sample Partially Completed Decision Matrix

CRITERIA ➤	Criterion 1	Criterion 2	Criterion 3	Criterion 4	Criterion 5	Total Score
	Importance to our internal school community students/ teachers (e.g., students, teachers, staff members)	Importance to our external school community (e.g., parents, employers, etc.)	We understand our goals and what we want to achieve in this area; it is part of our strategic plan	Probability for successful change in this area within 1 year is high	——	
OPTIONS ▼	Combined weight = 4.0	Combined weight = 1.2	Combined weight = 2.0	Combined weight = .80	Combined weight = ___	Enter rank times weight totals across all columns
1. Extend and restructure the school year	Consensus rank: 3 $3 \times 4.0 = 12.0$	5 $5 \times 1.2 = 6.0$	2 $2 \times 2.0 = 4.0$	——	——	
2. Redefine and integrate science, math, and technology curriculum and instruction	5 $5 \times 4.0 = 20.0$	4 $4 \times 1.2 = 4.8$	4 $4 \times 2.0 = 8.0$			
3. Institute site-based management	2 $2 \times 4.0 = 8.0$	2 $2 \times 1.2 = 2.4$	3			
4. ——	1 $1 \times 4.0 = 4.0$	3 $3 \times 1.2 = 3.6$	5			
5. ——	4 $4 \times 4.0 = 16$	2 $2 \times 1.2 = 2.4$	4			

5. Multiply weight times rank in each box.
6. Total the score in each box to find the option that best meets your criteria.

Remember that the value of this exercise is not just to get "the answer." There may be valid commonsense reasons to select one option over another, regardless of the score. The value of the decision matrix is in assisting the analysis, discussion, and best thinking of a team as to why a particular decision is selected and what criteria were used to select it.

Selecting the Benchmarking Team

The ideal benchmarking team consists of a team leader and five to six team members who are the most qualified people to understand, advocate, and implement change in the arena selected. Do *not* select team members based on time availability (i.e., who has the time to do this); rather, use the following criteria.

First, list all of the functions and people affected by the selected process. The top person (e.g., superintendent, department head, assistant principal, etc.) most directly involved in and accountable for the process (the "process owner") usually—but not necessarily—serves as the team leader. The most important function of the top administrator is to be a "champion" of the team by following its work, providing necessary resources, and removing barriers for the work.

Avoid duplication. Do an organizational scan of existing committees and groups that are already working on related issues. Pull team members from these groups.

Next, consider the skills and attributes required for an effective team and use these criteria to help you select members.

- Subject matter expertise
- Leadership ability and respect of peers
- Good communication skills
- Risk taker
- Interview skills
- Analytical skills

Stop Here and Complete Exercise 3.2

EXERCISE 3.2:
Identifying Team Members

Use the criteria just discussed to list the ideal benchmarking team for your project. See Table 3.4 for a suggested layout.

Table 3.4 Worksheet: Identify Team Members

Team leader   _____

Members   _____

                                   _____

                                   _____

                                   _____

                                   _____

Writing a Team Charter
to Plan Your Project

When the benchmarking team has been selected, one of its first tasks is to write a team charter.

Why Write a Team Charter?

A team works best when everyone involved understands its purpose and goals. The most frequent problems that teams encounter include the following:

- Lack of agreement on the purpose of the work
- Switches in direction
- Lack of common definitions of success for the team's work
- Feelings held by members that the project is too big or inappropriate
- Excessive questioning of each decision
- Lack of knowledge or resources to deal with the issue

Most planning failures and team problems can be traced to confusion about the purpose, expected outcomes, authority, resources, or time lines of the team. Take as much time as necessary to clarify these issues up front, among and between team members and management.

Stop Here and Complete Exercise 3.3

EXERCISE 3.3:
Writing a Team Charter

Follow the directions contained in the sample worksheet shown in Table 3.5 to draw up a team charter.

Table 3.5 Worksheet: Our Team Charter

Team Name   Date

List Team Members

Project Definition and Goals
Define the benchmarking project. List a few of your major goals for the project. Be certain that all members agree on the operational definitions of key words.

How will we determine whether or not our benchmarking project is successful, short term and long term?

Who are the internal and external customers of the project?
List the individuals or groups, inside and outside of the school, who will receive the results of your work.

Decision making and authority level
How will the team make decisions? To whom does the team report; what sign-offs are necessary?

Resources
Do we have adequate time, money, and access to information to complete this project? Are the right people on the team?

Time Lines
Estimate how long the project will take, including key reporting dates. How often will the team meet? For how long? How often will the team meet?

4

═══════

Studying and Documenting
Your Current Practice

First know thyself.
  —Source unknown

THE PURPOSE OF THIS CHAPTER IS
for the team to study the practice in their school or school
system.

IN Chapter 1, the basic questions of a benchmarking study
were introduced. This chapter addresses the questions listed
in the right-hand column in Table 4.1: It's about knowing
yourself—what you are doing, how you are doing it, and how well
you are doing it.

To answer these questions, this chapter leads the team
through the following concepts and exercises:

■ Establishing performance measures: What are the indicators of success in this practice?

Table 4.1 Benchmarking Methodology Answers These Questions

Know Your School	Know Their School
What are you doing?	What are they doing?
How are you doing it?	How are they doing it?
How well are you doing it?	How well are they doing it?

- Building a process chart to develop a shared body of knowledge about what currently happens in your school's or school system's selected benchmarking area
- Analyzing the root causes of problems that occur in your process

This knowledge will enable you to ask the right questions of your benchmarking partner, bring the right information home, and make the right changes in your own process.

Getting Started

Ask People in Your School to Describe the Following Procedures

- How a new curriculum is developed and implemented
- How computers are introduced in the classroom
- How professional development is planned and deployed
- How a math lesson is integrated into a science lesson
- How a student is disciplined
- How a budget is formulated—or any other of the major work processes that occur each day

Then ask, "How do you define *success* in that new curriculum or in our professional development process or in the way we discipline students?"

Chances are that people think they know how work gets done in their school and that "studying the obvious" is a waste of time. When a team begins an analysis of the process and opportunities for improvement in that process, however, members are always surprised by their lack of knowledge, their degree of agreement, or both as to what really happens in any given process. They are surprised as well by how different members define success and the variety in views about why various problems occur.

Establishing Performance Measures

How do you know how well you are currently performing in your selected benchmarking practice? What results are you looking for? What data would you look for to indicate *success, excellence,* or *needs improvement?*

Although educators often claim that best practices are subjective and indefinable, the fact is that school practices are constantly studied and ranked by foundations, accreditation agencies, state departments, and—increasingly and most important—by internal and external customers. Admittedly, the methods and data used to create these rankings are often flawed, but excellence can be identified and analyzed. Teachers, parents, employers, and students generally know when a process is performing poorly and that there is a better way of doing things; they simply lack the tools, methods, and authority to make it better.

Exercise 4.1 in this chapter will help your team identify the indicators of how well your school or school system is currently performing and decide what data and measures to use in the study. *Indicators* are the measures of specific objective events and occurrences that provide information about the quality of a particular aspect of your school. Performance measures answer one of the essential benchmarking questions previously outlined: How well are we doing it compared with how well they are doing it? Benchmarking is essentially about closing the performance gap between you and the "best." Before you can close that gap, it needs to be defined. In later chapters, you will write questions for your benchmarking partner and determine how to collect their performance measures. First you need to define your own performance measures.

Establishing these measures can be a relatively easy and straightforward team task, with readily available data. If, for example, the team is benchmarking a specific instructional area and determines that standardized test scores represent the performance measures, those data are easy to obtain and display.

On the other hand, establishing performance measures can be one of the most difficult tasks facing the benchmarking team. Members might not agree on indicators because they have different ideas about how to define success. Or data to help the team determine how well the school or school system is performing in a specific area might either be buried somewhere or not available because it has never been collected.

For example, *parental involvement* is a major issue in most schools, but indicators and data regarding it can be difficult to agree on and obtain. What should be measured: the number of parent volunteers in the school, the percentage of families that are parent-teacher association members, the percentage of parents that show up for parent-teacher conferences, the number of parents who come to the school's open house? There are many such questions.

Likewise, if you are benchmarking a practice that is new to your school, such as a school-to-work apprentice program, you will need to define the gap you are trying to close between your current performance and your desired performance. What are the indicators in this case: the number of graduating students that obtain jobs at a baseline wage, the number of employers who hire and retain the student apprentices?

Determining performance measures for a practice such as the use of educational technology requires more than simply counting the number of computers per classroom. The team has to decide what results they are looking for in educational technology and how to measure those results (the performance measures).

The instructions for Exercise 4.1 include several tips and guidelines to facilitate this activity. The team should spend whatever time is necessary to discuss, reach consensus, and collect data on performance measures.

Stop Here and Complete Exercise 4.1

EXERCISE 4.1:
Establishing Performance Measures

This exercise can take 15 minutes or 2 hours depending on the degree of consensus among team members and the availability of data that the team believes is necessary to describe current performance. Looking over the examples of performance measures shown in Table 4.2 is a good preparation.

Table 4.2 Examples of Performance Measures

Discipline and Violence Prevention
>   The number of incidents involving violence
>   The number of repeat offenders
>   The extent to which students and teachers identify violence as a factor that inhibits learning
>   And so on

Foreign Language Curriculum and Instruction
>   Number of students who pass a level X proficiency test in Spanish by the X grade
>   Number of graduating students who are able to waive foreign language requirements in postsecondary institutions
>   Number of students who take advanced placement foreign language courses
>   And so on

School-Based Management
>   The number of items within the school's allocated budget that can be changed without higher approval
>   The number of suggestions from school-based teams that were implemented without central office approval
>   The extent to which hiring decisions are made within the building
>   The number of hours (days, weeks) dedicated to central office reports
>   And so on

NOTE: These examples are for illustration purposes only. It is important for the team to develop its own indicators.

1. Ask the following question and record members' responses on a flip chart. Remember that you are determining broad, overall measures, not micromeasures. Do not focus on either individuals or individual problems in the process.

   ■ What are the key indicators of how we are currently performing?

Probe Questions

   ■ How do we know how we are doing?
   ■ What data do we collect to measure quality?
   ■ Who collects these data and who shares it?
   ■ What results are we looking for?
   ■ What indicators will we use to search for the best?

☞ *TIP: Go back to Chapter 3, Exercise 3.1, and review why you selected this area for benchmarking. Why is it important to your school? Why are internal customers, external customers, or both currently dissatisfied with the process?*

---

2. Look for common themes among team members' ideas and rewrite the measures to reflect these themes. There is room for more than one measure when trying to reach consensus.

☞ *TIP: Avoid prolonged discussions of educational philosophy that can emerge in this exercise. Bring the discussion back to the purpose of the benchmarking project: to learn together how to improve.*

---

3. Determine how to articulate your current performance using the measures you have established. What data currently exist that

confirm your performance (e.g., staff or parent surveys, accreditation reports, test scores, reports to the state, etc.)?

If no hard data exist in a specific area, determine whether or not it is necessary to collect it to describe your current performance. Consider the following questions:

- Are observations and estimates sufficient to describe your performance? For example, "Approximately 50 parents had unfulfilled requests for this service last year." "We estimate that 10% of our faculty uses computer-assisted instruction." "According to our discussions with the community college, X is the primary reason our students take remedial classes after graduation."
- Will your description of your current performance be open to challenge by others in the school community without hard data?
- Will you be able to adequately describe the performance gap between your school and your partner's school without hard data?

4. If the team determines that more data are necessary, develop a "who, when, where, and what" plan for collecting it.

Understanding What
You Do and How You Do It

Each day, millions of people go to work because they have "stuff" to do. Whether they work in a school, a hospital, a printing company, or a biotechnology lab, they have stuff to get done each day. Ask a colleague to meet for coffee after school and a common response is, "I can't today, because I have too much stuff to do."

An educator has a lesson to teach, a student to discipline, a seminar to attend, a report card to write, a test to correct, a parent to meet—some of the work stuff performed each day in schools everywhere.

Although this work appears to be performed in isolation behind a classroom door or the principal's office door, it is actually performed within a context of policies, procedures, methods, and materials that have been developed in the school. For example, how the lesson is taught depends to a large extent on the curriculum, materials, and methods that are supplied to the teacher; how a student is disciplined is directly related to the school's established discipline policies and procedures; whether a teacher's seminar is valuable or worthless depends very much on how professional development is planned and implemented in the school; and so forth. Understanding the "whats and hows" of work in your school involves analyzing how people, policies, procedures, materials, and methods all feed into the collective results of your work.

Before you can understand how and why another school is getting excellent outcomes, you need to thoroughly understand your own practices. Otherwise, you will miss key information in your benchmarking study and be unable to understand why another school is achieving such good results. Both good and bad results occur the way they do because a process—including policies, people, procedures, materials, methods, and equipment—has evolved that is producing these results. Willingness to investigate why current practices are what they are and to question how they can be improved sets the stage for benchmarking.

The following example illustrates how these components "feed" success or failure in the familiar process of introducing and implementing a change in your school or school system. Consider any of the practices in your school, from assessment to foreign language instruction to professional development to violence prevention and discipline. A change—a new way of performing this work—is introduced. What are some of the ways that policies, procedures, materials, methods, and equipment determine the success or failure of this change process?

- The school board or superintendent, unilaterally or with many stakeholders, establishes a policy that is either coherent or incoherent.
- The policy is then clearly explained, or not, to the principal.
- The principal then establishes, or doesn't establish, clear procedures and methods for the teachers.

- The teachers are, or are not, trained in these procedures and either given or not given good materials and equipment to use in the classroom.
- In the classroom, the procedure is then either used, rewarded, and assessed or discarded and forgotten.

In all process analysis, the purpose is *not* to assign blame or point fingers at any individual or group. The purpose is to determine, "How can we do it better—where can we improve the policies, procedures, and materials?"

In this chapter, it is vital to keep your eye on the benchmarking goal: to learn and adapt a best *practice,* not a best *person.* People in the school or school system come and go, but the "we have always done it this way" mentality lingers because familiar practices are comfortable even if they are flawed.

Stop Here and Complete Exercise 4.2

EXERCISE 4.2:
Building a Process Chart

This exercise gives your team the opportunity to brainstorm, discuss, and reach consensus on what your current practice looks like, whether you are benchmarking a specific curriculum and instruction area, such as science, or your professional development practices. The end result of the exercise will be a visual picture of the components that go into your selected benchmarking area. The instructions provide detailed steps on building a process chart. This chart will be invaluable in comparing your practices to the practices of your benchmarking partner. The similarities and the differences will be easy to recognize and define, instead of being vague and confusing.

Imagine that a stranger has come to your school on an urgent mission and must return home and duplicate, as precisely as possible, your practices. To fulfill the mission, the main characteristics of what you do and how you do it must be crystal clear. Your team's job is to provide enough information about your policies, procedures, methods, and materials and how they move through your school or school system so that the stranger can go home and duplicate your process.

☛ *TIPS before you begin:*

The purpose of this exercise is to build a visual picture of the way things work in your school, not the way they ought to work. Answer the questions based on current reality.

Do not try to analyze your problems in this exercise. Simply get "the picture" on the board. Your visitor is not interested in knowing your problems but, rather, what you do. Problem analysis will come later.

Tape large flip sheets or butcher paper on the wall for work space and have plenty of Post-it notes on hand.

Save your work for further use.

---

1. Write each of the following four questions on the flip sheets, leaving space under each question for several Post-it™ notes.

   ■ What are the origins of your current practice? Describe the main policies and procedures that determine how the current practice works in your school.
   ■ What are all of the ways that information about these policies and procedures is disseminated throughout the school community to all stakeholders? What are the steps? Who hands the information off to whom? What meetings, bulletins, training, notices, and so forth are in place for every group, inside and outside of the school?

Table 4.3 Random Sample of Brainstorming Notes—Practice Under
Study: Foreign Language Curriculum and Instruction

The state requires 2 years of foreign language for high school graduation.	We have four levels of study from I (introduction) to IV (advanced). Students must move through the levels sequentially.	The language lab is open from 2 to 4 p.m. on Wednesday.
In ninth grade, students decide whether to study Spanish or French.	The department head selects the textbooks with a review committee.	Parents receive information at an eighth-grade open house.
Five students study German at the community college.	Foreign language classes are 55 minutes a day, 5 days a week.	
Students spend 3 hours a week in the language lab.	All foreign language teachers are certified in one language.	

- What are the critical materials and equipment (e.g., books, curriculum, manuals, technology) that are used in the process?
- What else does your visitor need to know about your current practice to be able to duplicate it?

2. Have each team member write his or her responses to the first question on a Post-it note. Post all notes randomly under the question. See Table 4.3 for an example of this step. Give the team the following instructions:

- Print your ideas clearly so that other members can read them.
- Avoid one-word responses, because a single word will not convey meaning to your visitor or to other team members. For example, a one-word note, such as "training," will not mean anything to your team, whereas a note saying, "All teachers get 4 hours of training on X method," is very clear.
- Use *verbs* wherever possible because they clarify your ideas.

3. Working as a team, move the notes around so that duplicate ideas or ideas that seem to go together are placed in one column and other groups of ideas are placed in other columns. For example, notes such as "call students' parents," "meet with students' parents," and "agree on a course of action with students' parents" would all be placed in the same column.

You will have varying numbers of columns depending on how many duplicates and how many themes emerge from team members. Some notes may be "stand-alones" and not fit into any column. Do not discard the stand-alones until you determine whether or not they represent a major theme you want to include.

4. Consolidate each column into a single main idea that represents one of the "consensus answers" to the question.

5. Repeat steps one through four for each remaining question.

Examining the
Root Cause of Process Problems

All of us have experienced failure due to process problems: Even though we worked very hard, we were unable to perform well because the procedures, training, or equipment supplied to us for our work made it impossible to deliver satisfactory results. Our own talents and efforts are significant, but we also need *enablers:* all the conditions that are supplied to us in the process. Every input in the process counts toward the end result.

Problem identification and root cause analysis help the team look beyond the symptoms of the problem to deeper causes. This information will be invaluable when you design the questionnaire for your benchmarking partner because you will not overlook important enablers in your partner's practices. You will obtain more thorough and specific information about how they addressed the problems, issues, and barriers.

In Exercise 4.1, you established performance measures to determine how well your school or school system is performing overall in a specific area. Success indicators are also helpful, however, in analyzing and articulating problems and mistakes that occur in components and steps in the process.

The next step is to examine problems that currently occur in your process. These problems are typically expressed as time, cost, outcome, customer satisfaction, accuracy, or dependability issues in comments such as the following: "It takes too long." "It costs too much." "Teachers hate it." "Nobody pays attention to it." "It only works under certain conditions."

Again, the purpose for examining causes is improvement, not finger pointing. It is important to look beyond individual behaviors and personality traits when examining root causes. Consider the difference between the two following statements: "A required sign-off by the assistant superintendent results in delay" versus "It goes to Joe for a sign-off; he can't make a decision, so months go by." Joe may be gone next year, and the real issue may be an unnecessary step—a required sign-off—rather than Joe's inability to make a quick decision.

Common Process Problems

- This takes too long and results in delays—a *time* measure.
- This is too expensive; it costs too much—a cost measure.
- This usually results in mistakes and errors that have to be redone—an *accuracy* measure.
- The teachers (or parents or students) hate this—a *customer satisfaction* measure.
- This is unreliable: Sometimes it works; sometimes it does not—a *dependability* measure.

Stop Here and Complete Exercise 4.3

EXERCISE 4.3:
Problem Identification and Root Cause Analysis

1. Review the process chart you developed in Exercise 4.2. Ask, "Are there any problems that occur frequently in this area or this step?" or "Are there items on this chart that rarely produce good outcomes or that rarely meet the expectations of teachers (or parents or students)?"

Articulate the problem by writing it on the flip chart sheet using Table 4.4 as a guide.

Table 4.4 Problem Identification Form

Problem/Barrier/Issue #1	Problem/Barrier/Issue #2
_____	_____
_____	_____
Why?	*Why?*
Because:	Because:
Why?	*Why?*
Because:	Because:
Why?	*Why?*
Because:	Because:

2. Ask of each problem, up to three times, "Why?" and answer, "Because _____." Stop asking Why? when you reach consensus on the underlying cause of the problem.

The following are examples of potential root causes:

- The procedure is not understood.
- No training has been provided on how to do this.
- No time has been set aside to learn it.
- It's not important to anyone.
- The school board requires it.
- No money has been appropriated for it.
- There is no follow up to the training.
- We don't have the materials.
- There are no incentives.
- There is no space.
- State law mandates it.
- There are too many interruptions.

☞ *TIP: The team should move through this exercise rather quickly and not agonize over each item. This is not an in-depth problem analysis exercise. Rather, the purpose is to identify your problems and barriers so that you can ask the right questions to learn how your benchmarking partner addressed these barriers or solved these problems.*

5

Identifying and Establishing
Your Benchmarking Partner

Learn—and steal—from the best.
                    —Anonymous

THE PURPOSE OF THIS CHAPTER IS
to assist you in

- defining the ideal benchmarking partner profile,
- conducting research to locate that partner, and
- establishing the ground rules for the partnership.

The Characteristics of an
Ideal Benchmarking Partner

The two most common mistakes in selecting a partner can be traced to the criteria a team establishes for its search: establishing criteria that do not matter and overlooking criteria that do matter.

Criteria That Do Not Matter

Selecting criteria that do not matter usually results from the mistaken belief that the partner "has to look just like us" for the study to be successful. In the corporate world, industries cut across all lines to find partners. Black and Decker benchmarked Hallmark, Lexus, and McDonald's to determine how to best launch new products in the market. Motorola benchmarked Domino's Pizza to shorten the time between order receipt and delivery of its cellular phones. Swiss Bank Corporation benchmarked overnight package delivery companies to design a problem resolution process.

Although this guide assumes that most of your initial benchmarking studies will be within the education sector—school to school or system to system—the lesson from industry is that your partner *does not* have to look just like you for the project to be successful.

The purpose of benchmarking is to make larger and faster improvements than you could ordinarily make in your school. This requires creativity—getting "outside the box" and having open minds. Private schools, magnet schools, and private learning centers should not be automatically excluded as possible partners.

You are looking for breakthrough ideas. Determining how to adapt and fit these ideas in your school comes later in the project during the analysis and implementation planning phases addressed in Chapters 7 and 8.

Numbers of students, test scores, wealth of the community, demographics, the composition of the student body, budget, and governance characteristics may or may not be important depending on the topic you have chosen. Use these characteristics as criteria only if they are integral to the practice you are studying. For example, community demographics may be important to a bilingual education project but not to a project concerned with team teaching and integrated curriculum.

Criteria That Do Matter

Benchmarking is the search for and adaptation of best practices. The ability to validate the success of a partner's practice is clearly an important criterion. Inadequate research on the actual performance measures used by your potential partner can lead you to a school with great public relations hype but very little substance for you to take home.

Budget limitations may dictate a geographic criterion if you are planning site visits to your partner. State laws that mandate or prohibit certain practices may negate a particular transfer of practices and dictate the need for an in-state partner.

Do not overlook the possibility of a benchmarking partner in your own district. More and more large businesses find best practices at different locations within their own corporate structure. Sometimes a best practice is around the corner.

Stop Here and Complete Exercise 5.1

EXERCISE 5.1:
Select Criteria for Choosing Your Partner

1. Brainstorm a list of characteristics you consider important in a benchmarking partner. List them on a flip chart. Refer to Table 5.1 for some examples.

   If you generate six or fewer criteria and the team generally agrees on them, you can skip step 2. If you have more than six criteria or there is not consensus on the team as to what is important, go on to step 2.
2. Prioritize the list by having each team member rank each item from 6 (highest in importance) to 1. Add the numbers for a consensus ranking of the most important criteria. If you have more than six criteria, drop the lowest-ranked ones.

Table 5.1 Sample List of Criteria

According to our research, this school has achieved the success indicators we think are important.

Their success can be validated from at least two separate sources.

The principals in their system have generally the same budget and governance responsibilities as our principals.

The school is within driving distance from our community.

And so on.

Conducting Research
to Locate Your Partner

After you have established criteria for choosing your partner, the search for one that meets those criteria begins. There is no shortage of education associations, journals, and computer information on best practices. Some resources for your search are the following:

- The National Diffusion Network (555 New Jersey Avenue NW, Washington, D.C. 20208, 202-219-2134)
- Professional associations, such as the Association for Supervision and Curriculum Development, the National Science Teachers Association, the National Council of Teachers of Mathematics, and the International Reading Association
- ERIC Search—Education Resource Information Center: an on-line index of education research and resources
- Conferences and conference proceedings
- Education journals
- Schools of Education at colleges and universities
- State Departments of Education
- U.S. Department of Education
- Consultants
- Your own staff

At this stage in the process, the following two things are important:

1. A thoughtful analysis of potential partners (rather than an "off-the-cuff" selection of a school that "someone heard was good")
2. The participation of every team member in the research and final selection of your partner

By putting together a responsibility matrix (Exercise 5.2, to follow), you will ensure that you have cast a wide net and involved the entire team. The matrix is a visual picture of who has agreed to do what job and when. It prevents the wheel spinning and lack of accountability that often characterize group work.

Stop Here and Complete Exercise 5.2

EXERCISE 5.2:
The Responsibility Matrix

1. Referring to Table 5.2, a sample responsibility matrix, for the layout, list all pertinent specific research tasks down the left side of a large flip chart page (e.g., calls, literature search, faculty interviews, etc.).
2. List the committee and staff members across the top of the page.
3. Indicate with an X who is responsible for each item and enter the date by which it is to be done.

If one person on the team has several Xs on the chart and another team member has none, the team can discuss the situation at this point and make any indicated adjustments.

Table 5.2 Sample Responsibility Matrix

Research Task	Name: Dan	Name: Jean	Name: Phil	Name: Nancy	Name: Helen
Task 1: Call National Diffusion Network for information		X Sept. 20			
Task 2: Conduct a literature search at the University	X Oct. 3				X Oct. 3
Task 3: Call Department of Education			X Sept. 20		
Task 4: Survey staff for suggestions				X Oct. 3	
Task 5: Validate the performance of potential partners		X Oct. 15	X Oct. 15		
Task 6: ERIC search					

Contacting a Potential
Partner and Forming Agreements

A letter to the school or school system's top management, followed by phone contact, is usually the best method of initiating a partnership. Many schools with best practices are inundated with requests for visits and information and often receive little or no feedback on the results. The time and energy expended on these run-of-the-mill visits can cause reluctance to participate unless there is some payoff for your partner. In most cases, the opportunity to learn more about benchmarking will be a sufficient incentive for partnership.

In your initial contact, be sure to

- indicate why you have selected them for the area you are studying (e.g., your initial data suggest that they are a leader in the field);
- identify sources of information (e.g., recommendations, articles, etc.);
- give a brief explanation of your benchmarking process to convey your sincerity and intention to complete an in-depth study;
- give a brief explanation of what your expectations are of their contribution of time and data to the study;
- mention that your benchmarking is going to be intellectually rigorous, not of the "school tourism" variety;
- indicate that they, too, will benefit from the study (if, in fact, you feel this is true); and
- specify a day that you will call them to answer questions and, you hope, secure their participation.

Making the
Final Selection of Your Partner

After you have collected your research information, narrow the field down to three or four likely candidates. Be certain that the performance of these schools has been validated through a secondary source or a call to the school or district and not merely selected from an article in a journal. Evaluate each candidate against your criteria to select the best one.

6

Developing a Questionnaire
and Site Visit Guidelines

Only the right questions yield the right answers.
— Anonymous

THE PURPOSE OF THIS CHAPTER IS
to guide you through a process that will lead to a productive site visit in which you ask the right questions and bring home the right information to plan improvements in your school.

Are Site Visits Always Necessary?

More and more organizations are conducting successful benchmarking projects via phone, fax, and E-mail. Travel expenses can, in fact, be prohibitive. Site visits have several advantages, however, particularly when you are just beginning benchmarking; the directness of face-to-face interviews, the opportunity to hear from several players, and direct observation versus "filtered information" yield better information than phone inter-

Table 6.1　Benchmarking Methodology Answers These Questions

What are you doing?	What are they doing?
How are you doing it?	How are they doing it?
How well are you doing it?	How well are they doing it?
Why are we getting our results?	Why are they getting their results? (What are the conditions and enablers?)

SOURCE: Xerox Corporation. Used by permission.

views. Regardless of the method used to collect information from your partner, you need to spend time on your questionnaire to ensure that you collect what you need.

Table 1.3 in Chapter 1, shown here as Table 6.1, outlined the basic premises of benchmarking that result in self-knowledge and an understanding of why and how the "best of the best" got that way. You completed the questions about your school in Chapter 4; it is now time to move on to Part B—understanding your partner.

Complete the following before you begin writing questions for your partner:

- Collect all of the documentation generated by the team in previous chapters. Review your process chart and problem analysis from Chapter 4: Good questions come from your own self-study.
- Brainstorm a general list of items you need to know from your partner, including performance measures.
- Put together a profile of your partner from the information already collected or easily available by phone. (You won't want to waste time during the site visit asking

Table 6.2 Basic Benchmarking Questions

Briefly describe the history of this practice in your school. What were the major decisions, motivations, and milestones that led to your current practice?

What are the criteria you use to define excellence in this practice? How do you measure the quality outcomes and progress in this area?

Describe the steps and the components of your current practice, including the people, policies, procedures, materials, and equipment that "feed" it.

How does information and training about the practice flow to all of the stakeholders in the school?

How much and what type of training do you provide for the various personnel involved in the process?

What were your largest barriers to implementing the practice, and how did you overcome them?

How do you handle cost and resource allocation?

What steps and actions have given you the best return in performance improvements?

---

about size, demographics, or other easily obtained facts about the school.)

- Consider the types of questions available to you:

  - Open-ended—respondents answer in their own words in essay form (see the examples in Table 6.2)

Table 6.3 Questionnaire Guidelines

Begin with easy, open-ended questions that allow your partners to talk about their successful practice and establish a comfort level with your team.

Allow space for writing responses.

Be clear about asking "what is," not "what should be."

Request data that confirm performance, such as time, cost, reliability, customer satisfaction, and outcome measures.

Try not to phrase questions in a way that suggests a response or leads to speculation or opinion.

If you want factual answers, do not ask hypothetical questions; "who, when, what, and how" questions generally elicit factual information.

Be cautious about vague words such as *generally* or *several.*

Avoid questions that are too personal or demanding.

- Forced-response choices, such as "yes" or "no"
- Multiple choice—respondents select among options, which may include a blank for "other"
- Rank or scaled questions, such as, "On a scale of 1 to 5, how important is *X*?"

■ Review the basic benchmarking questions shown in Table 6.2 and the questionnaire guidelines shown in Table 6.3.

Because of competition and bottom-line profit issues, private industry gives considerable attention to benchmarking ethics, industrial espionage, and the misuse of proprietary information. Educators enjoy a significant advantage in this arena; most schools are proud to share "how-tos" with others without fear of economic consequences. Nevertheless, it is important to establish ground rules regarding the use of the information you are requesting. Be considerate of any personal or political concerns of your partner in releasing the information in articles, forums, or other public documentation.

Stop Here and Complete Exercises 6.1 and 6.2

EXERCISE 6.1:
Developing a Questionnaire for Your Partner

1. Review your self-study information and brainstorm a list of critical information you need to collect from your partner. Also, review the basic benchmarking questions shown in Table 6.2.
2. Reviewing the types of questions possible (open-ended, multiple choice, etc.), determine the best way to obtain the information you need.
3. Draft your questions.

EXERCISE 6.2:
Reviewing the Questions

Ask the following questions about the draft questions you have written:

- Are they clear and understandable? Check for ambiguity.
- Is it possible to answer them in a reasonable period of time?
- Will they guide your team to the knowledge it seeks?
- Have you used your process map and problem analysis to be certain you have covered pertinent issues?
- Are there questions that will probably not be of real use to you, which could be deleted?

■ Are there people outside your team who should review the questions or serve as a "test run" panel?

Developing Logistics and a Strategy for Your Visit

Although the entire team needs to be involved in developing the questionnaire, it is not necessary for all members to conduct the site visit. Two or three members are usually sufficient.

Before Confirming Your Visit

Your partner needs to know well in advance what your expectations are for the visit. Answer the following questions so that you can relay the appropriate information to your partner:

■ Do you want specific people, by name or title, to answer specific questions? For how long?
■ Do you want to meet with an implementation team at the school? For how long?
■ Do you want to visit particular areas or spend most of the time in meetings? (Be clear about your lack of interest in a "dog-and-pony show.")
■ What documentation would you like to have ahead of time?
■ Will you record the interviews? Ask permission.
■ What information can you bring or send that may be of value to your partner?

Before Your Actual Visit

■ Plan an agenda with time lines.
■ Assign responsibilities such as the following among those conducting the visit:

– Who will be responsible for asking questions and doing follow-ups?
– Who will be responsible for monitoring the time?
– Who will take notes? (Written documentation of observations is important, even if you record the interviews.)

Immediately Following Your Visit

It is *extremely important* to have a debriefing session with the site visit team as soon as possible after the visit—the same evening if possible—to discuss and capture the main ideas. Do not wait more than a day or two after the visit to move to the next chapter; memories are short.

7

Analyze—
Recommend—
Communicate

*Individuals learn all the time and yet there is no
organizational learning. But if teams learn, they become
a microcosm for learning throughout the organization.*
—Peter Senge (quoted in Belden
et al., 1993, p. 1)

THE PURPOSE OF THIS CHAPTER IS
to assist the benchmarking team in

- analyzing and summarizing what they learned from the
  project,
- selecting the best ideas for implementation in their
  school system, and
- communicating its recommendations to the school
  community.

There are three steps in this process:

1. Confirming and articulating the performance gap between your school and your partner's school.
2. Evaluating and prioritizing the improvement ideas for use in your school.
3. Preparing a storyboard to share your study with the school community.

Confirming and Articulating the Performance Gap

The first step in your analysis is to confirm and articulate the performance gap between your outcomes and those of your partner. What data and information did you collect that substantiate your partner's outcomes? Good data help you make a case for changing the status quo. Without data, skeptics will immediately "beat up" on your study.

There is a tendency to look for weaknesses in your partner ("They are not as good as we thought they were") and defend your own practices ("We are better than we thought"). Indeed, inadequate data (covered in Chapter 4), inadequate research (discussed in Chapter 5), or both can result in lack of measurable goals or false expectations of your partner's performance. Be honest in your assessment and use objective data to illustrate the performance gap.

Stop Here and Complete Exercise 7.1

EXERCISE 7.1:
Articulating the Performance Gap

Using Table 7.1 as a guide, write a short and easy-to-understand statement that illustrates the performance gap between you and your partner.

Table 7.1 Articulating the Performance Gap

How well are *we* doing it? Use your performance measures from Chapter 4.

How well are *they* doing it? Use the information collected during your site visit.

Evaluating and Prioritizing
Improvement Ideas for Your School

At this point in your project, you have important information
to work with. You have analyzed your own way of doing things and
the root cause of problems you encounter in a practice that is very
important to your school's customers and improvement goals. You
have confirmed that your partner is getting better results than
you are, and you have asked the right questions to determine what
they do and how they do it. Now your job is to assess what is
important and adaptable to your school. Benchmarking is not
copying; it is learning and adapting.

The following four ground rules will help you avoid mistakes
in this process of learning and adapting:

1. Commit to the analysis process before either dismissing
   or selecting ideas for recommendation.
2. Recognize that you are entering the "sell" phase of
   your work in which gaining acceptance of your study

is critical. Be strategic in your invitations to others to participate in the analysis process.

3. Do not get bogged down in implementation details. At this point, your task is to develop a list of broad recommendations based on your findings. Implementation planning is far more detailed and is covered in the final chapter.

4. Keep an open mind.

A common mistake at this point in the project is to jump to conclusions about your partner's practices and about what will or will not work in your school. Important information is often "dismissed and dumped" because it is overwhelming, unanticipated, or too challenging to the status quo.

All benchmarking teams encounter surprises in their studies, such as unanticipated data and information about their partner's practices that do not fit with the mental picture they have been drawing during the project.

Likewise, all benchmarking teams feel overwhelmed by the inevitable conclusion that, regardless of what practice they are studying, it is linked to numerous other processes in the system. For instance, curriculum development is linked to instructional practices that are linked to professional development practices that are in turn linked to budget practices and on and on. Most teams understand the complexity and interrelationship of these processes from their own self-study covered in Chapter 4. Nevertheless, they are often unprepared for the power of these connections and the implications for changing the status quo.

Determining Key People to Add to Your Team to Evaluate and Prioritize Improvement Ideas

Now is the time to consider whether surprises or system effects have expanded the scope of your study to the point where you need to bring in some key new people to assist you in evaluating your improvement ideas. *Key people* are those managers (process owners) who will be directly affected by your recommen-

dations and responsible for implementing changes and monitoring results. Sometimes benchmarking teams find that their study
has expanded into processes beyond the scope of members' expertise. It is wise—for both political and information reasons—to
reach beyond the team for that experience.

Indeed, not all information and ideas from your study will be
equally useful to you. Some of the ideas you bring home will be
less relevant to your improvement goals; others will be impossible
to implement, at least in the short run, due to political or budget
barriers in your school. The following exercises will help your
team make recommendations that are well thought-out, well
documented, and less open to challenge from others in the school
community.

Stop Here and Complete Exercise 7.2

EXERCISE 7.2:
Evaluating and Prioritizing
Improvement Ideas for Use in Your School

A similar process was used in putting together a decision matrix in Exercise 3.1 in Chapter 3; see Table 3.2 on p. 24 for an example of this tool.
Use Table 7.2 as a layout guide for this exercise.

1. List all of the ideas that emerged from your study down the left
    side of your matrix. Include your partner's action steps, enablers
    (e.g., training, scheduling revisions), and inputs (e.g., materials,
    advisory groups, technology).
2. Establish criteria for determining which ideas to recommend to
    your school community. Common criteria include the following:

Table 7.2 Analysis Matrix Layout

Ideas	Criterion 1	Criterion 2	Criterion 3	Criterion 4	Total
1.					
2.					
3.					
4.					
5.					

- The extent to which implementing the improvement idea will close the performance gap (i.e., its effect on key results)
- The likely degree of buy-in from internal customers
- The likely degree of buy-in from external customers
- Feasibility within a certain time frame (establish your criterion as 6 months, 1 year, 2 years, etc.)
- The extent to which the item is fiscally feasible (i.e., cost considerations)

3. By consensus, rank how well each improvement idea meets each criterion. If there are eight items, the item that best meets the criterion receives an 8; the item that least meets it receives a 1.

4. Add the scores of each idea across its row of criteria; analyze your resulting data. Which items received very high scores? Are these your priority recommendations? Which items received very low scores? Should they be dropped from your list or put on the "back burner"? Why or why not?

Use common sense as well as the scores to reach your conclusions. Remember that the purpose of this matrix is not to yield decisions for you on a purely numerical basis but to allow you to present a thoughtful analysis of your study to stakeholders and demonstrate that your recommendations are based on careful analysis. You will be able to make the following statements:

- We learned about many good ideas.
- We analyzed these ideas according to factors in our own school.
- We understand that there are big potential gains for us in some of these ideas as well as difficulties and barriers to making them work in our school or school system.

Communicating Your Project: Telling a Story

Your team has generated a great deal of information, data, analysis, and recommendations. Now your task is to sort out and put in sequence the information that will be relevant, interesting, and meaningful to your audiences, whether they are hearing your story in a school auditorium or reading it in a special bulletin.

Through the ages and in all cultures, one of the best methods of communication has been to tell a story: Who did what, why and when did they do it, and what did they learn? Stories accompanied by visual aids are particularly compelling. Cartoons, for example, are popular because they use both words and pictures to communicate in a very concise way. Storyboards are used worldwide by teams to communicate their work to internal and external stakeholders.

Some general guidelines for developing a storyboard include the following:

- Be concise; sort the relevant from the irrelevant and the highlights from the details.
- Have fun and add humor to your storyboard with cartoons, quips, or pictures. Do not bore your audience.
- Keep it visual; wherever possible use charts, graphs, and bullet points instead of narrative.
- Pretend that you are the customer of the presentation. Consider what you would want to know if you were on the receiving end of the presentation.

Introduce the Team

A fun magazine picture or visual that represents your team name and purpose can grab people's attention. Likewise, team members can be introduced with "middle names" that represent a positive personality trait or special talent that they brought to the team (it's important that there are no put-downs here). For instance, there could be Dane "Get the Data" Smith, Sue "Hot Idea" Jones, and so on.

Describe the Rationale for the Issue Selected for Benchmarking

Review your decision matrix in Chapter 3 and summarize the main reasons this topic was selected. Use quotes or data that illustrate customer dissatisfaction with the status quo.

Present a Picture of the Current Situation

Drawing from data you collected, your process chart, and your root cause analysis, emphasize any breakthrough ideas that resulted from this process analysis. Avoid comments that place blame on any individuals or group in your school. Use humor, if possible, to illustrate the "we have always done it this way even if it doesn't make sense" syndrome.

Explain Why You Selected the Particular School or Organization to Benchmark

Use your criteria and research summary to illustrate the thinking that went into your selection of a particular partner.

Summarize Your Research Questions and Answers

Show what you set out to learn and what, in fact, you did learn.

Present Your Recommendations

- Articulate the performance gap.
- Share a summary of your matrix analysis of recommendations.
- Be nonthreatening and recognize that you do not have all the answers.
- Invite broad participation in the implementation phase.

Stop Here and Complete Exercise 7.3

EXERCISE 7.3:
Preparing a Storyboard of Your Project

Following the storyboard guidelines just outlined and listed in Table 7.3, use creative adaptation to tell your own team story.

Table 7.3 Storyboard Guidelines

Introduce the team.

Describe the rationale for the issue selected for benchmarking.

Present a picture of the current situation using collected data, your process chart, and root cause analysis.

Explain why you selected the particular school or organization to benchmark.

Summarize your research questions and answers.

Present your recommendations.

8

Developing
Implementation Plans

Quality is never an accident; it is always the result of high intention, sincere effort, intelligent direction and skillful execution. It represents the wise choice of many alternatives.

—Will Foster (quoted in McAlindon, 1992, p. CQ5)

THE PURPOSE OF THIS CHAPTER IS
to assist you by providing basic guidelines for implementing benchmarking recommendations.

YOU have completed your study, communicated the results, and built support in the school community for improvement. Much time and energy has been invested in your benchmarking project, but the real payoff is in actually implementing your recommendations.

This guide is not a definitive road map for managing the human, political, and financial dimensions of change. Every school

69

and school system has its own culture and methods of instituting change; there is reference material on the subject in the Suggested Reading list. The basics of implementation in this chapter include the following four sections:

- Establishing a structure for implementation
- Overcoming barriers and pitfalls
- Applying the plan–do–check–act cycle
- Developing an action plan

Establishing a
Structure for Implementation

Who is responsible for implementing the recommendations of the benchmarking team and monitoring progress? How should the implementation be structured?

The answers depend on the scope of your recommendations and the extent to which administrators, faculty, and staff members who will be directly involved in implementation are represented on the benchmarking team. If the team consists of top management working on a strategic issue that only top management can address, the team can move forward with its own implementation plan.

Typically, however, the recommendations will affect many people who have not been part of the team and whose buy-in and expertise are critical to success. If you have followed the steps in the previous chapter, you have been building consensus for change by bringing appropriate people into the loop during the recommendation process. In the implementation phase, the circle will widen further. Remember that everything looks easy to the people who don't have to do it themselves. Therefore, the people in your school or school system who actually do the work and will be responsible for the results must be the ones involved in this final phase. Again, depending on the scope of the recommendations, entire new teams may be formed for implementation. Industry often refers to these implementers as *performance teams*.

It is clear that someone from the administration must be designated to coordinate and remove barriers for the implementation team or teams. This person has typically been part of the original study and has the vision, authority, and leadership to help implement the recommendations.

Overcoming Barriers and Pitfalls

Force-Field Analysis

The first step in overcoming barriers and pitfalls is to recognize and articulate what they are. Force-field analysis is an important tool for teams to understand the powers that are driving the school toward the desired change (the helping factors) and those that are driving the school away from the desired change (the hindering factors). Experts in change management have long maintained that energy flows toward the status quo and change occurs only if the helping factors are strengthened and the hindering factors are reduced. A good force-field analysis serves as a reality check and yields information about human, financial, political, and system barriers needing to be addressed in your action plan.

Stop Here and Complete Exercise 8.1

EXERCISE 8.1:
Force-Field Analysis

1. In a phrase, describe the issue under discussion at the top of a flip chart sheet. What is the desired change-action-goal?

Table 8.1 Force-Field Analysis: Example

Driving Forces	Restraining Forces
We have the data to demonstrate that it works	Uncertain whether we can get money in the budget for training
The superintendent supports it	The X parent organization may oppose it
Teachers are dissatisfied with the current process	It is perceived as a fad

2. Divide the flip chart paper in half. List all of the helping factors driving your school toward the change in the left-hand column and all the hindering factors driving your school away from the desired change in the right-hand column. Refer to Table 8.1 for the suggested layout and example.
3. Determine the most important driving and restraining forces. Teams often generate long lists of factors on each side. To determine the most significant factors, ask each member to rank the factors from 6 (high) to 1 (low) in terms of their perceived effects regarding the desired change. The simplest process is to have members write their rankings beside the factors on the flip chart. Add each group of numbers to find the team total. Those factors with the highest totals will be targeted in your planning grid (Exercise 8.2).

Applying the Plan–Do–Check–Act Cycle

If force-field analysis illustrates that your recommendations are putting your school on "resource or change overload," do not be discouraged. Realities of time and resource allocation, politics, and human resources may dictate a scaling back of activities and recommendations. This can be frustrating for participants who envisioned immediate large-scale changes. The key is to make certain that your benchmarking study is activated instead of sitting on a shelf. The plan-do-check-act (PDCA) cycle shown in

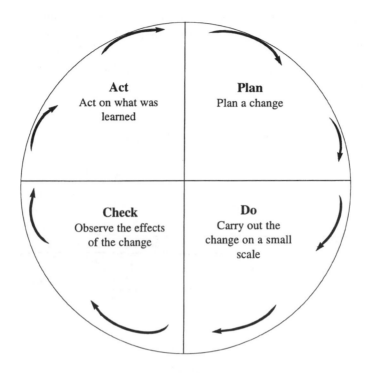

Figure 8.1. The Plan-Do-Check-Act Cycle

Figure 8.1, a universal management process and a fundamental principle of quality, provides a context to consider how your recommendations can be scaled back to "pilot project" status.

Educators are not strangers to the PDCA cycle: They *plan* a lesson—*do* the lesson—*check* to ascertain whether students have learned the material—and *act* on that knowledge by moving forward or reviewing the lessons. It is easy for educators to understand this principle because it is used constantly in the classroom.

Applying the same principle to broader process changes in the workplace is more difficult, however. Whether introducing new technology, changing a curriculum, or extending the school year, too often the plan step is faulty (a truck could be driven through the holes in the plan), the check step—to ascertain whether or not

the changes actually result in the desired improvements—is to-
tally overlooked, and no one is clear about what information to act
on. Understanding and applying the PDCA cycle to implementation planning can energize a team discouraged by the barriers it
is encountering.

Developing an Action Plan

Implementation planning is less formidable if the components
(what, who, when, how) are visually displayed and completed by
team consensus. Necessary questions to ask include the following:
What are our goals? What activities need to happen to reach our
goals? Who will perform these activities and in what time frame?
What resources are necessary to successfully accomplish the activities? How will we measure success? The *planning grid* brings
all of these elements together into a useful tool for your team.

Stop Here and Complete Exercise 8.2

EXERCISE 8.2:
The Planning Grid

For complex projects, you may need several grids, one for each recommendation.

1. Copy the planning grid shown in Table 8.2 on a flip chart or
   butcher paper to keep it visible to the team.
2. Define the goal you are trying to achieve through the activities.
   When you reach consensus on the goal, fill in the goal statement
   on the grid.

Table 8.2 Planning Grid

Benchmarking Team Recommendation: _____				
Our Goal: _____				
Activity-Task	Who? (who else?)	Target Date	Resources Required	Desired Outcome
1.				
2.				
3.				
4.				

3. Using Post-it notes, brainstorm all of the activities and tasks that have to be done to reach your goal. Post the notes randomly on a sheet near the grid. *Use verbs:* This is action planning.
4. Combine duplicates and notes that go together to form a task that would have a common deadline or purpose. For example, "notify parents," "meet with parents," and "get feedback from

parents" might be combined into a single task labeled, "obtain parental input."

5. Fill in the grid according to the general sequencing of the activities. The first activity would go in Slot 1, the second in Slot 2, and so on. Do not agonize over sequencing. Many times, activities occur simultaneously or the order is very difficult to determine because one activity depends on the successful completion of another activity. Use the slot numbers as a general guideline only.

6. Fill in the remainder of the grid: the *who, when, resources,* and *outcomes* details.

7. Have the team review the planning grid by answering the following questions:

   ■ Do the activities adequately address the priority factors in our force-field analysis?
   ■ Will they strengthen the driving forces and reduce the barriers?
   ■ If all of these tasks and activities are successfully completed, will we reach our goal? Have we omitted important activities?

9

In Conclusion . . .

THE PURPOSE OF THIS CHAPTER IS
to provide you with two wrap-up activities that will signif-
icantly affect future benchmarking projects in your school:

- A time to celebrate, capture, and record the team's
  learning
- Recognition of the team and team members by the
  superintendent, principal, and school board

A group that has worked together as long and as hard as
your benchmarking team needs to come to closure in very
specific ways. Whether the project is perceived as wildly
successful or as a flop, simply disbanding after the final meeting
is not adequate closure for either the team members or for the
school community that invested resources in the project.

Celebrating, Capturing,
and Recording the Learning

Before the team disbands, a special time should be set aside
for members to talk about the entire experience and add *Things*

Table 9.1 Things We Learned and Recommendations to New
Benchmarking Teams

What went well in this project? What aspects of the project were especially
worthwhile and meaningful?

What did not go well in this project? Where did problems, difficulties, and frus-
trations emerge? What would we have done differently if we had it to do over?

If a new benchmarking team is formed at the school, we definitely recommend
the following:

We Learned and Recommendations to New Benchmarking Teams
to the documentation that will be saved.

To reinforce benchmarking as a learning experience, members
need to share their feelings, observations, and improvement ideas
for future teams. This gathering should be in a relaxed, "debriefing" atmosphere and, if possible, combined with recognition of
each member's contributions to the team. No other items should
be on the agenda.

If you do not have an outside facilitator for this meeting, it is
a good idea to rotate the facilitation and recording responsibilities
so all members can participate. For example, each member can
take turns recording on the flip chart. Be certain to assign responsibility for documenting the meeting and adding it to the team
report.

The probe questions shown in Table 9.1 help teams to "capture
the learning." All aspects of the team process and the benchmarking process from beginning to end should be considered. Items not
to be included are individual personalities or behaviors. Remember to phrase and record responses in a way that will make sense

to people who were not a part of your team and want to learn from your experience (i.e., avoid code words and "inside information" that only you understand).

Team Recognition

On a final note, enthusiasm for future team projects—including further benchmarking studies—will largely depend on the degree to which the initial team is encouraged and recognized by the top management in the school system, including the school board. Use meetings, bulletins, and special events to show appreciation for the team's efforts.

References

American Productivity and Quality Center. (1993). *The benchmarking management guide.* Portland, OR: Productivity Press.

Belden, G., Hyatt, M., & Ackley, D. (1993). *Towards the learning organization.* St. Paul, MN: Author.

Boxwell, R. J. (1994). *Benchmarking for competitive advantage.* New York: McGraw-Hill.

Camp, R. C. (1989). *Benchmarking: The search for industry best practices that lead to superior performance.* Milwaukee, WI: Quality Press (ASQC).

Malcolm Baldrige National Quality Award. (1994). *The Malcolm Baldrige National Quality Award criteria.* Gaithersburg, MD: National Institute of Standards and Technology.

McAlindon, H. (1992). *Commitment to quality.* Lombard, IL: Celebrating Excellence.

Pinellas County Schools. (1994). *Superintendent's quality challenge.* Largo, FL: Author.

Suggested Readings

American Association of School Administrators. (1991). *Introduction to total quality for schools: A compilation of articles on the concepts of total quality management and W. Edwards Deming.* Arlington, VA: Author.

American Association of School Administrators. (1992). *Creating quality schools.* Arlington, VA: Author.

American Association of School Administrators. (1994). *Quality goes to school: Readings on quality management in education.* Arlington, VA: Author.

Bonstingl, J. J. (1992). *Schools of quality: An introduction to total quality management in education.* Alexandria, VA: Association for Supervision and Curriculum Development.

Byrnes, M. A., Cornesky, R., & Byrnes, L. (1992). *The quality teacher: Implementing total quality management in the classroom.* Bunnell, FL: Cornesky.

Covey, S. R. (1989). *The seven habits of highly successful people.* New York: Simon & Schuster.

Covey, S. R. (1991). *Principle-centered leadership.* New York: Simon & Schuster.

Fields, J. C. (1994). *Total quality for schools: A guide for implementation.* Milwaukee, WI: Quality Press (ASQC).

Glasser, W. (1990). *The quality school.* New York: Harper & Row.

GOAL/QPC. (1992). *The memory jogger for education: A pocket guide of tools for continuous improvement in schools.* Methuen, MA: Author.

GOAL/QPC. (1993a). *The educators' companion to the memory jogger plus +.* Methuen, MA: Author.

GOAL/QPC. (1993b). *Total quality management in education* [Video-supported training series]. Methuen, MA: Author.

McClanahan, E., & Wicks, C. (1993). *Future force—Kids that want to, can, and do!* Chino Hills, CA: PACT Publishing.

McCormick, B. L. (1993). *Quality and education: Critical linkages.* Princeton Junction, NJ: Eye on Education.

Murgatroyd, S., & Morgan, C. (1993). *Total quality management and the school.* Buckingham, UK: Open University Press.

Neuroth, J., Plastrik, P., & Cleveland, J. (1992). *The total quality management handbook.* Lansing, MI: On-Purpose Associates.

Rinehart, G. (1992). *Quality education.* Milwaukee, WI: Quality Press (ASQC).

Sarason, S. B. (1990). *The predictable failure of educational reform: Can we change it before it's too late?* San Francisco: Jossey-Bass.

Schargel, F. P. (1994). *Transforming education through total quality management: A practitioner's guide.* Princeton Junction, NJ: Eye on Education.

Schenkat, R. (1993). *Quality connections: Transforming schools through total quality management.* Alexandria, VA: Association for Supervision and Curriculum Development.

Scholtes, P. (1994). *The team handbook for educators.* Madison, WI: Goiner Associates, Inc.

Siegel, P., & Byrne, S. (1994). *Using quality to redesign school systems: The cutting edge of commonsense.* San Francisco: Jossey-Bass.

Walton, M. (1986). *The Deming management method.* New York: Perigee.

Watson, G. (1992). *The benchmarking workbook: Adapting best practices for performance improvement.* Cambridge, MA: Productivity Press.